THE ULTIMATE GUIDE TO THE

DECLARATION OF INDEPENDENCE

David Hirsch and Dan Van Haften

SB

Savas Beatie

California

www.thestructureofreason.com

First edition, first printing
ISBN-13: 978-1-61121-373-7
eISBN: 978-1-61121-374-4

Library of Congress Cataloging-in-Publication Data

Names: Hirsch, David, 1947- author. | Van Haften, Dan, author.
Title: The ultimate guide to the Declaration of Independence / by David Hirsch and Dan Van Haften.
Description: First edition. | El Dorado Hills, California : Savas Beatie, 2017. | Includes bibliographical references and index.
Identifiers: LCCN 2017018233| ISBN 9781611213737 (pbk : alk. paper) | ISBN 9781611213744 (ebk.)
Subjects: LCSH: United States. Declaration of Independence--Criticism, Textual.
Classification: LCC E221 .H57 2017 | DDC 973.3/13--dc23
LC record available at https://lccn.loc.gov/2017018233

SB

Published by
Savas Beatie LLC
989 Governor Drive, Suite 102
El Dorado Hills, California 95762

Phone: 916-941-6896
Email: sales@savasbeatie.com
Web: www.savasbeatie.com

Savas Beatie titles are available at special discounts for bulk purchases in the United States by corporations, institutions, and other organizations. For more details, please contact Special Sales, P.O. Box 4527, El Dorado Hills, CA 95762, or you may email us at sales@savasbeatie.com, or visit out website at www.savasbeatie.com for additional information.

The Object of the Declaration

"[T]he object of the Declaration of Independance...[was] to place before mankind the common sense of the subject...[in] terms so plain and firm, as to command their assent, and to justify ourselves in the independant stand we [were] compelled to take." *Letter from Thomas Jefferson to Henry Lee, May 8, 1825*

Thomas Jefferson, by John Trumbull

Contents

Jefferson Made the Draft   1

The Discovery   3

The Structure of Reason Colorized   5

How Does a Proposition Mean?   8

The Six Elements of a Proposition

    1. Enunciation   10

    2. Exposition   12

    3. Specification   14

    4. Construction   16

    5. Proof   20

    6. Conclusion   24

Logical Development   26

Contents (continued)

"A Performance of Itself"   28

Hear All About It   34

Focus on Facts   36

The Greatest Question was Decided   41

"I Cannot Live Without Books"   46

The Masterpiece   49

Adams Made the Argument to Congress   53

Timeline   58

Endnotes   61

Index   68

Jefferson Made the Draft

On June 7, 1776, four days before the Continental Congress named a five-person committee to draft the Declaration of Independence, Richard Henry Lee proposed a resolution:

> *Resolved*, That these United Colonies are, and of right ought to be, free and independent States, that they are absolved from all allegiance to the British Crown, and that all political connection between them and the State of Great Britain is, and ought to be, totally dissolved.
>
> That it is expedient forthwith to take the most effectual measures for forming foreign Alliances.
>
> That a plan of confederation be prepared and transmitted to the respective Colonies for their consideration and approbation.[1]

The resolution led to the June 11, 1776, appointment of John Adams, Thomas Jefferson, and three others to a committee to draft the Declaration of Independence.[2] On August 6, 1822, 46 years after the Declaration, John Adams wrote former U.S. Senator from Massachusetts, Timothy Pickering, about its initial draft:[3] "Jefferson proposed to me to make the draught."

> Adams: I said, "I will not."
>
> Jefferson: "You should do it."

Adams: "Oh! no."

Jefferson: "Why will you not? You ought to do it."

Adams: "I will not."

Jefferson: "Why?"

Adams: "Reasons enough."

Jefferson: "What can be your reasons?"

Adams: "Reason first—You are a Virginian, and a Virginian ought to appear at the head of this business. Reason second—I am obnoxious, suspected, and unpopular. You are very much otherwise. Reason third—You can write ten times better than I can."

Jefferson: "Well," said Jefferson, "if you are decided, I will do as well as I can."

Adams: "Very well. When you have drawn it up, we will have a meeting."[4]

The Discovery

What made Jefferson's writing "ten times better"? A paragraph published in 1918 that compared Abraham Lincoln to Thomas Jefferson led to our discovery of the Declaration's six element structure.[5] Ohio Judge R. M. Wanamaker asked in *The Voice of Lincoln*:

> Where did he [Lincoln] get this order which he habitually followed in his discussions on law or government? He does not definitely advise us. Neither do any of his biographers. It is, however, more than passing strange that Lincoln's early acquaintance with, and study of, the Declaration of Independence brought him directly and intimately in touch with this method of presentation and argument. That Declaration of Independence is naturally divisible into those same three parts, declaration, demonstration, dedication. It is most natural for us to presume that Lincoln, who studied and quoted the Declaration of Independence more frequently than any other American statesman of his own time, or any other, should have been strikingly impressed with the logical order so plainly and powerfully put in the Declaration of Independence, by his great prototype, Thomas Jefferson.[6]

Judge Wanamaker was at least looking for method and structure. He missed the prize. He did not sense or know about the six elements of a proposition Jefferson and Lincoln both used.[7] The Declaration of Independence crisply demarcates into the six elements of a proposition.

In 1954, Thomas Jefferson biographer Dumas Malone also missed the prize regarding the Declaration's parts. Malone asserted:

> THE PAPER that had been adopted by Congress and proclaimed from Georgia to New Hampshire can be roughly divided into four parts: a preamble, a philosophical paragraph, a list of charges against the King, and at the end the actual declaration of independence—including the resolution adopted on July 2.[8]

Within six-element structure, the Declaration blended facts with pinpoint logic to confirm a hypothesis.

The Structure of Reason Colorized

The Declaration of Independence neatly fits into a six element pyramid. Colorized pyramids show relationships among the elements. Brown is factual foundation. Green is logical direction. Red is argument. Think of the six elements of a proposition as a scientific method for persuasive writing.

The Declaration of Independence is special. Examination of its elements reveals how. Brown, green, and red conceptual guides highlight the purpose of each element. Color lights up the Declaration like an X-ray or an MRI.

Brown factual foundation associates with the Given, Exposition, and Construction. Green logical progression associates with the Sought, Specification, and Conclusion.

The first four elements flow into the Proof (argument). The Conclusion flows out from the Proof. Argument is red. Argument is like fire. Timing, important for all the elements, is particularly important for the Proof.

The Declaration of Independence rises to a higher level when you understand brown, green, and red generally, and the elements specifically. We demonstrate how the Declaration's six parts explain, persuade, and prove.

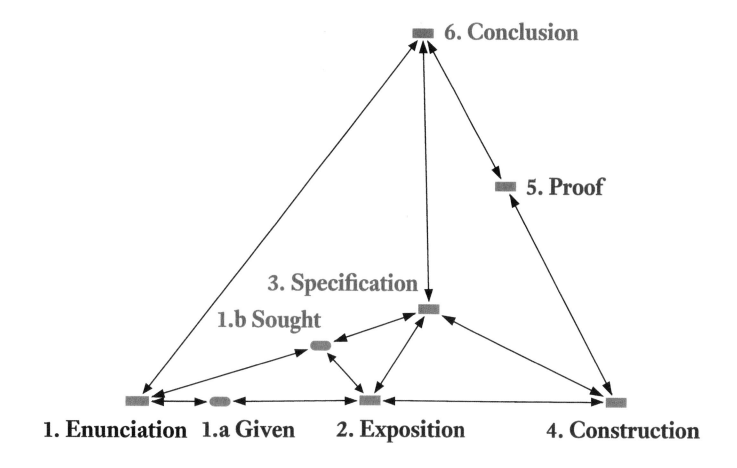

6. Conclusion

5. Proof

3. Specification

1.b Sought

1. Enunciation   1.a Given   2. Exposition   4. Construction

How Does a Proposition Mean?

At the beginning of his 1959 classic, *How Does a Poem Mean?*, John Ciardi wrote:

> A poem is a formal structure in which many elements operate at the same time. In analysis, each element must be discussed separately…Analysis is never in any sense a substitute for the poem. The best any analysis can do is to prepare the reader to enter the poem more perceptively. By isolating for special consideration some of the many simultaneous elements of the poem, analysis makes them more visible in one sense, and less interesting in another. It is up to the reader, once the analysis is completed, to re-read the poem in a way that will restore the simultaneity and therefore the liveliness and interest of the poetic structure. The only reason for taking a poem apart is that it may then be put back together again more richly…The usual question one hears of poetry is "What does a poem mean?" I am interested rather in "How" the poem means, how it goes about being a performance of itself.[9]

The six elements of a proposition enable one to peer into Thomas Jefferson's mind to see how he built the structured, logical demonstration known as the American Declaration of Independence. That structure provides precise location for the words, phrases, and sentences within.

Ciardi observed: "A poem exists in time. The first line comes first, the others follow in their order to the last line, and there is no other order in which the lines can be read."[10]

So it is with a demonstration according to the six elements. Logical order is fixed. Everything is essential. Linear in presentation, it all operates at the same time.

The structured logic of the Declaration makes great poetry. Words perfectly timed lead to persuasion. All within "a performance of itself".

The Six Elements of a Proposition

1. Enunciation – "The enunciation states what is given and what is being sought from it."[11]

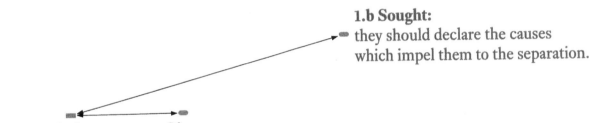

1.b Sought:
they should declare the causes
which impel them to the separation.

1. Enunciation

1.a Given:
When in the Course of human events, it becomes necessary
for one people to dissolve the political bands which have
connected them with another, and to assume among the
powers of the earth, the separate and equal station to which
the Laws of Nature and of Nature's God entitle them, a
decent respect to the opinions of mankind requires that

The Enunciation answers the question: Why are we here?

The Enunciation's Given references "the Laws of Nature and of Nature's God" as an ultimate standard.

A Given includes indisputable, basic facts.

The Enunciation's Sought is, "they should declare the causes which impel them to the separation."

A Sought is a relatively neutral statement of the general issue.

The complete Enunciation:

> [**Given**] When in the Course of human events, it becomes necessary for one people to dissolve the political bands which have connected them with another, and to assume among the powers of the earth, the separate and equal station to which the Laws of Nature and of Nature's God entitle them, a decent respect to the opinions of mankind requires that [**Sought**] they should declare the causes which impel them to the separation.

2. Exposition – "The exposition takes separately what is given and prepares it in advance for use in the investigation."[12]

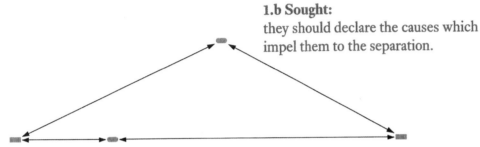

1.b Sought:
they should declare the causes which impel them to the separation.

1. Enunciation

1.a Given:
When in the Course of human events, it becomes necessary for one people to dissolve the political bands which have connected them with another, and to assume among the powers of the earth, the separate and equal station to which the Laws of Nature and of Nature's God entitle them, a decent respect to the opinions of mankind requires that

2. Exposition:
We hold these truths to be self-evident, that all men are created equal, that they are endowed by their Creator with certain unalienable Rights, that among these are Life, Liberty and the pursuit of Happiness. That to secure these rights, Governments are instituted among Men, deriving their just powers from the consent of the governed, That whenever any Form of Government becomes destructive of these ends, it is the Right of the People to alter or to abolish it...

The Exposition answers the question: What do we need to know relating to what is Given?

The Exposition factually expands from the Given, to state that, "…all men are created equal, that they are endowed by their Creator with certain unalienable Rights, that among these are Life, Liberty and the pursuit of Happiness." The facts in an Exposition should be largely indisputable. Its full text is:

> We hold these truths to be self-evident, that all men are created equal, that they are endowed by their Creator with certain unalienable Rights, that among these are Life, Liberty and the pursuit of Happiness. That to secure these rights, Governments are instituted among Men, deriving their just powers from the consent of the governed, That whenever any Form of Government becomes destructive of these ends, it is the Right of the People to alter or to abolish it, and to institute new Government, laying its foundation on such principles and organizing its powers in such form, as to them shall seem most likely to effect their Safety and Happiness.
>
> Prudence, indeed, will dictate that Governments long established should not be changed for light and transient causes; and accordingly all experience hath shewn, that mankind are more disposed to suffer, while evils are sufferable, than to right themselves by abolishing the forms to which they are accustomed.

3. Specification – "The specification takes separately the thing that is sought and makes clear precisely what it is."[13]

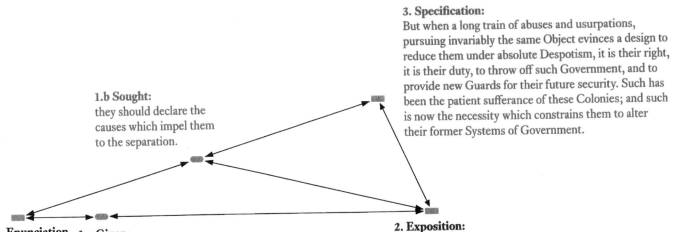

3. Specification:
But when a long train of abuses and usurpations, pursuing invariably the same Object evinces a design to reduce them under absolute Despotism, it is their right, it is their duty, to throw off such Government, and to provide new Guards for their future security. Such has been the patient sufferance of these Colonies; and such is now the necessity which constrains them to alter their former Systems of Government.

1.b Sought:
they should declare the causes which impel them to the separation.

1. Enunciation

1.a Given:
When in the Course of human events, it becomes necessary for one people to dissolve the political bands which have connected them with another, and to assume among the powers of the earth, the separate and equal station to which the Laws of Nature and of Nature's God entitle them, a decent respect to the opinions of mankind requires that

2. Exposition:
We hold these truths to be self-evident, that all men are created equal, that they are endowed by their Creator with certain unalienable Rights, that among these are Life, Liberty and the pursuit of Happiness. That to secure these rights, Governments are instituted among Men, deriving their just powers from the consent of the governed, That whenever any Form of Government becomes destructive of these ends, it is the Right of the People to alter or to abolish it...

The Specification answers the question: What must be resolved to achieve what is Sought?

A Specification is more precise than the Sought. The Sought was to declare the causes of the need to separate. The Specification is the precise hypothesis that will be proved, the need to immediately alter the system of government: "…such is now the necessity which constrains them to alter their former Systems of Government."

While a Specification can be stated in a partisan manner, it need not be. A Specification must be provable with facts and logic. The Declaration's Specification is:

> But when a long train of abuses and usurpations, pursuing invariably the same Object evinces a design to reduce them under absolute Despotism, it is their right, it is their duty, to throw off such Government, and to provide new Guards for their future security.

> Such has been the patient sufferance of these Colonies; and such is now the necessity which constrains them to alter their former Systems of Government.

4. Construction – "The construction adds what is lacking in the given for finding what is sought."[14]

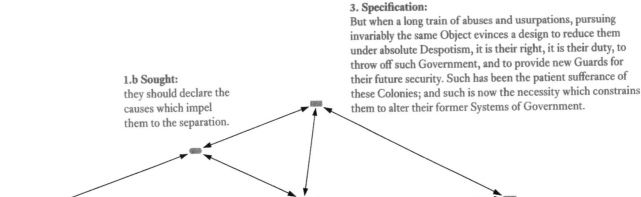

3. Specification:
But when a long train of abuses and usurpations, pursuing invariably the same Object evinces a design to reduce them under absolute Despotism, it is their right, it is their duty, to throw off such Government, and to provide new Guards for their future security. Such has been the patient sufferance of these Colonies; and such is now the necessity which constrains them to alter their former Systems of Government.

1.b Sought:
they should declare the causes which impel them to the separation.

1. Enunciation

1.a Given:
When in the Course of human events, it becomes necessary for one people to dissolve the political bands which have connected them with another, and to assume among the powers of the earth, the separate and equal station to which the Laws of Nature and of Nature's God entitle them, a decent respect to the opinions of mankind requires that

2. Exposition:
We hold these truths to be self-evident, that all men are created equal, that they are endowed by their Creator with certain unalienable Rights, that among these are Life, Liberty and the pursuit of Happiness. That to secure these rights, Governments are instituted among Men, deriving their just powers from the consent of the governed, That whenever any Form of Government becomes destructive of these ends, it is the Right of the People to alter or to abolish it…

4. Construction:
The history of the present King of Great Britain is a history of repeated injuries and usurpations, all having in direct object the establishment of an absolute Tyranny over these States. To prove this, let Facts be submitted to a candid world. He has refused his Assent to Laws, the most wholesome and necessary for the public good…

The Construction answers the question: How do the facts lead to what is Sought?

A Construction arrays facts in a manner that leads to argument in the Proof.

The last sentence in the first paragraph of the Declaration's lengthy, fact-based Construction states, "To prove this, let Facts be submitted to a candid world." The Declaration's Construction marshals facts. The arrayed facts are grievances against King George III:

> The history of the present King of Great Britain is a history of repeated injuries and usurpations, all having in direct object the establishment of an absolute Tyranny over these States. To prove this, let Facts be submitted to a candid world.
>
> He has refused his Assent to Laws, the most wholesome and necessary for the public good.
>
> He has forbidden his Governors to pass Laws of immediate and pressing importance, unless suspended in their operation till his Assent should be obtained; and when so suspended, he has utterly neglected to attend to them.
>
> He has refused to pass other Laws for the accommodation of large districts of people, unless those people would relinquish the right of Representation in the Legislature, a right inestimable to them and formidable to tyrants only.
>
> He has called together legislative bodies at places unusual, uncomfortable, and distant from the depository of their public Records, for the sole purpose of fatiguing them into compliance with his measures.

He has dissolved Representative Houses repeatedly, for opposing with manly firmness his invasions on the rights of the people.

He has refused for a long time, after such dissolutions, to cause others to be elected; whereby the Legislative powers, incapable of Annihilation, have returned to the People at large for their exercise; the State remaining in the mean time exposed to all the dangers of invasion from without, and convulsions within.

He has endeavoured to prevent the population of these States; for that purpose obstructing the Laws for Naturalization of Foreigners; refusing to pass others to encourage their migrations hither, and raising the conditions of new Appropriations of Lands.

He has obstructed the Administration of Justice, by refusing his Assent to Laws for establishing Judiciary powers.

He has made Judges dependent on his Will alone, for the tenure of their offices, and the amount and payment of their salaries.

He has erected a multitude of New Offices, and sent hither swarms of Officers to harrass our people, and eat out their substance.

He has kept among us, in times of peace, standing Armies without the Consent of our legislatures.

He has affected to render the Military independent of and superior to the Civil power.

He has combined with others to subject us to a jurisdiction foreign to our constitution, and unacknowledged by our laws; giving his Assent to their Acts of pretended Legislation:

For Quartering large bodies of armed troops among us: For protecting them, by a mock Trial, from punishment for any Murders which they should commit on the Inhabitants of these States:

For cutting off our Trade with all parts of the world: For imposing Taxes on us without our Consent: For depriving us in many cases of the benefits of Trial by Jury: For transporting us beyond Seas to be tried for pretended offences: For abolishing the free System of English Laws in a neighbouring Province, establishing therein an Arbitrary government, and enlarging its Boundaries so as to render it at once an example and fit instrument for introducing the same absolute rule into these Colonies: For taking away our Charters, abolishing our most valuable Laws, and altering fundamentally the Forms of our Governments: For suspending our own Legislatures, and declaring themselves invested with power to legislate for us in all cases whatsoever.

He has abdicated Government here, by declaring us out of his Protection and waging War against us.

He has plundered our seas, ravaged our Coasts, burnt our towns, and destroyed the Lives of our people.

He is at this time transporting large Armies of foreign Mercenaries to compleat the works of death, desolation and tyranny, already begun with circumstances of Cruelty & perfidy scarcely paralleled in the most barbarous ages, and totally unworthy the Head of a civilized nation.

He has constrained our fellow Citizens taken Captive on the high Seas to bear Arms against their Country, to become the executioners of their friends and Brethren, or to fall themselves by their Hands.

He has excited domestic insurrections amongst us, and has endeavoured to bring on the inhabitants of our frontiers, the merciless Indian Savages, whose known rule of warfare, is an undistinguished destruction of all ages, sexes and conditions.

5. Proof – "The proof draws the proposed inference by reasoning scientifically from the propositions that have been admitted."[15]

3. Specification:
But when a long train of abuses and usurpations, pursuing invariably the same Object evinces a design to reduce them under absolute Despotism, it is their right, it is their duty, to throw off such Government, and to provide new Guards for their future security. Such has been the patient sufferance of these Colonies; and such is now the necessity which constrains them to alter their former Systems of Government.

5. Proof:
In every stage of these Oppressions We have Petitioned for Redress in the most humble terms: Our repeated Petitions have been answered only by repeated injury. A Prince, whose character is thus marked by every act which may define a Tyrant, is unfit to be the ruler of a free people...

1.b Sought:
they should declare the causes which impel them to the separation.

1. Enunciation

1.a Given:
When in the Course of human events, it becomes necessary for one people to dissolve the political bands which have connected them with another, and to assume among the powers of the earth, the separate and equal station to which the Laws of Nature and of Nature's God entitle them, a decent respect to the opinions of mankind requires that

2. Exposition:
We hold these truths to be self-evident, that all men are created equal, that they are endowed by their Creator with certain unalienable Rights, that among these are Life, Liberty and the pursuit of Happiness. That to secure these rights, Governments are instituted among Men, deriving their just powers from the consent of the governed, That whenever any Form of Government becomes destructive of these ends, it is the Right of the People to alter or to abolish it...

4. Construction:
The history of the present King of Great Britain is a history of repeated injuries and usurpations, all having in direct object the establishment of an absolute Tyranny over these States. To prove this, let Facts be submitted to a candid world. He has refused his Assent to Laws, the most wholesome and necessary for the public good...

20

The Proof answers the question: How does the admitted truth confirm the proposed inference?

The proposed inference is the Specification.

To draw the proposed inference, the Declaration's Proof first argued what the Colonists did:

1) ...Petitioned for Redress ...;

2) ...warned them from time to time...;

3) ...reminded them of the circumstances...;

4) ...appealed to their native justice and magnanimity...; and

5) ...conjured [implored] them by the ties of our common kindred...

The Proof then argued what the King did not do.

Imperfectly timed argument loses credibility. Properly done, argument is credible and persuasive. Ideally, after the first four elements the reader anticipates the Proof:

In every stage of these Oppressions We have Petitioned for Redress in the most humble terms:

Our repeated Petitions have been answered only by repeated injury. A Prince, whose character is thus marked by every act which may define a Tyrant, is unfit to be the ruler of a free people.

Nor have We been wanting in attentions to our Brittish brethren. We have warned them from time to time of attempts by their legislature to extend an unwarrantable jurisdiction over us. We have reminded them of the circumstances of our emigration and settlement here. We have appealed to their native justice and magnanimity, and we have conjured them by the ties of our common kindred to disavow these usurpations, which, would inevitably interrupt our connections and correspondence.

They too have been deaf to the voice of justice and of consanguinity. We must, therefore, acquiesce in the necessity, which denounces our Separation, and hold them, as we hold the rest of mankind, Enemies in War, in Peace Friends.

With clear or admitted facts, the Declaration scientifically proved the Specification's hypothesis. A firm Conclusion resulted. Scientific reasoning drew the proposed inference. What was a hypothesis in the Specification became fact in the Conclusion.

The Declaration's Proof is set off from the Construction before it, and from the Conclusion after it. Argument is perfectly placed:

6. Conclusion – "The conclusion reverts to the enunciation, confirming what has been proved."[16]

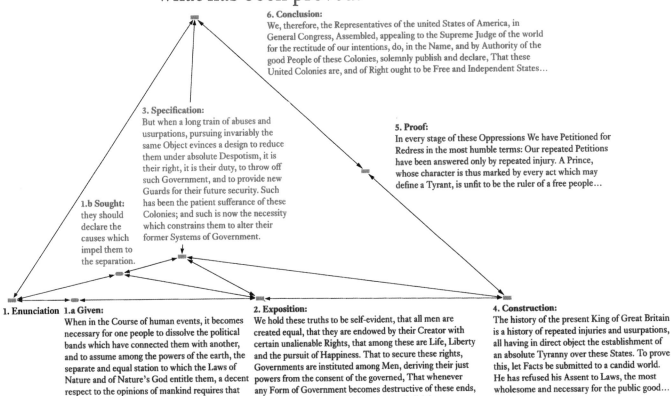

6. Conclusion:
We, therefore, the Representatives of the united States of America, in General Congress, Assembled, appealing to the Supreme Judge of the world for the rectitude of our intentions, do, in the Name, and by Authority of the good People of these Colonies, solemnly publish and declare, That these United Colonies are, and of Right ought to be Free and Independent States...

3. Specification:
But when a long train of abuses and usurpations, pursuing invariably the same Object evinces a design to reduce them under absolute Despotism, it is their right, it is their duty, to throw off such Government, and to provide new Guards for their future security. Such has been the patient sufferance of these Colonies; and such is now the necessity which constrains them to alter their former Systems of Government.

5. Proof:
In every stage of these Oppressions We have Petitioned for Redress in the most humble terms: Our repeated Petitions have been answered only by repeated injury. A Prince, whose character is thus marked by every act which may define a Tyrant, is unfit to be the ruler of a free people...

1.b Sought: they should declare the causes which impel them to the separation.

1. Enunciation

1.a Given:
When in the Course of human events, it becomes necessary for one people to dissolve the political bands which have connected them with another, and to assume among the powers of the earth, the separate and equal station to which the Laws of Nature and of Nature's God entitle them, a decent respect to the opinions of mankind requires that

2. Exposition:
We hold these truths to be self-evident, that all men are created equal, that they are endowed by their Creator with certain unalienable Rights, that among these are Life, Liberty and the pursuit of Happiness. That to secure these rights, Governments are instituted among Men, deriving their just powers from the consent of the governed, That whenever any Form of Government becomes destructive of these ends, it is the Right of the People to alter or to abolish it...

4. Construction:
The history of the present King of Great Britain is a history of repeated injuries and usurpations, all having in direct object the establishment of an absolute Tyranny over these States. To prove this, let Facts be submitted to a candid world. He has refused his Assent to Laws, the most wholesome and necessary for the public good...

The Conclusion answers the question: What was proved?

The Conclusion reverts to the Sought. The Declaration's Conclusion clearly declared separation based on a factual foundation logically presented. It resolved the issue generally presented in the Sought, and precisely presented as a hypothesis in the Specification.

> We, therefore, the Representatives of the united States of America, in General Congress, Assembled, appealing to the Supreme Judge of the world for the rectitude of our intentions, do, in the Name, and by Authority of the good People of these Colonies, solemnly publish and declare, That these United Colonies are, and of Right ought to be Free and Independent States; that they are Absolved from all Allegiance to the British Crown, and that all political connection between them and the State of Great Britain, is and ought to be totally dissolved;
>
> and that as Free and Independent States, they have full Power to levy War, conclude Peace, contract Alliances, establish Commerce, and to do all other Acts and Things which Independent States may of right do.
>
> And for the support of this Declaration, with a firm reliance on the protection of divine Providence, we mutually pledge to each other our Lives, our Fortunes and our sacred Honor.

Logical Development

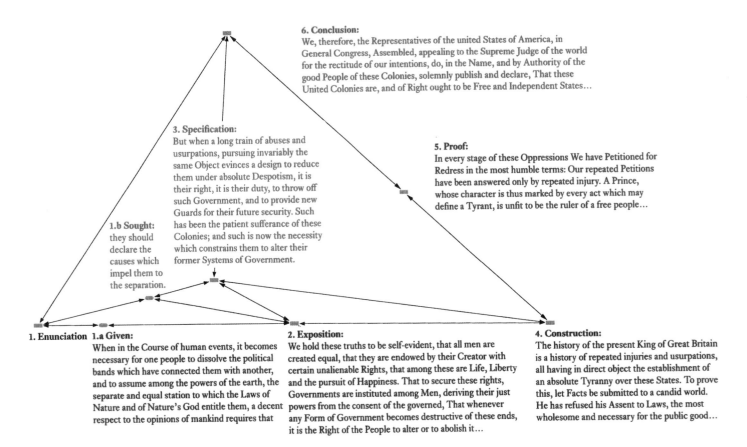

6. Conclusion:
We, therefore, the Representatives of the united States of America, in General Congress, Assembled, appealing to the Supreme Judge of the world for the rectitude of our intentions, do, in the Name, and by Authority of the good People of these Colonies, solemnly publish and declare, That these United Colonies are, and of Right ought to be Free and Independent States...

3. Specification:
But when a long train of abuses and usurpations, pursuing invariably the same Object evinces a design to reduce them under absolute Despotism, it is their right, it is their duty, to throw off such Government, and to provide new Guards for their future security. Such has been the patient sufferance of these Colonies; and such is now the necessity which constrains them to alter their former Systems of Government.

5. Proof:
In every stage of these Oppressions We have Petitioned for Redress in the most humble terms: Our repeated Petitions have been answered only by repeated injury. A Prince, whose character is thus marked by every act which may define a Tyrant, is unfit to be the ruler of a free people...

1.b Sought:
they should declare the causes which impel them to the separation.

1. Enunciation

1.a Given:
When in the Course of human events, it becomes necessary for one people to dissolve the political bands which have connected them with another, and to assume among the powers of the earth, the separate and equal station to which the Laws of Nature and of Nature's God entitle them, a decent respect to the opinions of mankind requires that

2. Exposition:
We hold these truths to be self-evident, that all men are created equal, that they are endowed by their Creator with certain unalienable Rights, that among these are Life, Liberty and the pursuit of Happiness. That to secure these rights, Governments are instituted among Men, deriving their just powers from the consent of the governed, That whenever any Form of Government becomes destructive of these ends, it is the Right of the People to alter or to abolish it...

4. Construction:
The history of the present King of Great Britain is a history of repeated injuries and usurpations, all having in direct object the establishment of an absolute Tyranny over these States. To prove this, let Facts be submitted to a candid world. He has refused his Assent to Laws, the most wholesome and necessary for the public good...

The Sought, Specification, and Conclusion show logical development (green). Development begins with a general statement of what is Sought: "...they should declare the causes which impel them to the separation." It progresses to a Specification that states a hypothesis: "...such is now the necessity which constrains them to alter their former Systems of Government." It ends with a Conclusion that confirms what was proved: "...all political connection between them and the State of Great Britain, is and ought to be totally dissolved..." This is the logical flow.

Logical development rests on fact (facts are brown: Given, Exposition, and Construction). The Given: "...the Laws of Nature and of Nature's God...," are presented as indisputable. The Exposition adds, "We hold these truths to be self-evident, that all men are created equal, that they are endowed by their Creator with certain unalienable Rights, that among these are Life, Liberty and the pursuit of Happiness." Facts arrayed in the Construction are precise grievances against King George III. The Construction marshals facts (admissible evidence) that lead to the Proof.

The Proof, red, is the second to last element. It contains perfectly timed argument with a foundation of largely indisputable fact, brown. Logical development (green) weaves around fact. Both fact and logic funnel through the Proof's argument to reach a self-evident Conclusion. The hypothesis (Specification) becomes fact.

"A Performance of Itself"

IN CONGRESS, July 4, 1776.

The unanimous Declaration of the thirteen united States of America,[17]

When in the Course of human events, it becomes necessary for one people to dissolve the political bands which have connected them with another, and to assume among the powers of the earth, the separate and equal station to which the Laws of Nature and of Nature's God entitle them, a decent respect to the opinions of mankind requires that they should declare the causes which impel them to the separation.

We hold these truths to be self-evident, that all men are created equal, that they are endowed by their Creator with certain unalienable Rights, that among these are Life, Liberty and the pursuit of Happiness. That to secure these rights, Governments are instituted among Men, deriving their just powers from the consent of the governed, That whenever any Form of Government becomes destructive of these ends, it is the Right of the People to alter or to abolish it, and to institute new Government, laying its foundation on such principles and organizing its powers in such form, as to them shall seem most likely to effect their Safety and Happiness. Prudence, indeed, will dictate that Governments long established should not be changed for light and transient causes; and accordingly all experience hath shewn, that mankind are more disposed to suffer, while evils are sufferable, than to right themselves by abolishing the forms to which they are accustomed. But when a long train of abuses and usurpations, pursuing invariably the same Object evinces a design to reduce them under absolute Despotism, it is their right, it is their duty, to throw off such Government, and to provide new Guards for their future security. Such has been the patient sufferance of these Colonies; and such is now the necessity which constrains them to alter their former Systems of Government. The history of the present King of Great Britain is a history of repeated injuries and usurpations, all having in direct object the establishment of an absolute Tyranny over these States. To prove this, let Facts be submitted to a candid world.

He has refused his Assent to Laws, the most wholesome and necessary for the public good.

He has forbidden his Governors to pass Laws of immediate and pressing importance, unless suspended in their operation till his Assent should be obtained; and when so suspended, he has utterly neglected to attend to them.

He has refused to pass other Laws for the accommodation of large districts of people, unless those people would relinquish the right of Representation in the Legislature, a right inestimable to them and formidable to tyrants only.

He has called together legislative bodies at places unusual, uncomfortable, and distant from the depository of their public Records, for the sole purpose of fatiguing them into compliance with his measures.

He has dissolved Representative Houses repeatedly, for opposing with manly firmness his invasions on the rights of the people.

He has refused for a long time, after such dissolutions, to cause others to be elected; whereby the Legislative powers, incapable of Annihilation, have returned to the People at large for their exercise; the

State remaining in the mean time exposed to all the dangers of invasion from without, and convulsions within.

He has endeavoured to prevent the population of these States; for that purpose obstructing the Laws for Naturalization of Foreigners; refusing to pass others to encourage their migrations hither, and raising the conditions of new Appropriations of Lands.

He has obstructed the Administration of Justice, by refusing his Assent to Laws for establishing Judiciary powers.

He has made Judges dependent on his Will alone, for the tenure of their offices, and the amount and payment of their salaries.

He has erected a multitude of New Offices, and sent hither swarms of Officers to harrass our people, and eat out their substance.

He has kept among us, in times of peace, standing Armies without the Consent of our legislatures.

He has affected to render the Military independent of and superior to the Civil power.

He has combined with others to subject us to a jurisdiction foreign to our constitution, and unacknowledged by our laws; giving his Assent to their Acts of pretended Legislation:

For Quartering large bodies of armed troops among us:

For protecting them, by a mock Trial, from punishment for any Murders which they should commit on the Inhabitants of these States:

For cutting off our Trade with all parts of the world:

For imposing Taxes on us without our Consent:

For depriving us in many cases of the benefits of Trial by Jury:

For transporting us beyond Seas to be tried for pretended offences:

For abolishing the free System of English Laws in a neighbouring Province, establishing therein an Arbitrary government, and enlarging its Boundaries so as to render it at once an example and fit instrument for introducing the same absolute rule into these Colonies:

For taking away our Charters, abolishing our most valuable Laws, and altering fundamentally the Forms of our Governments:

For suspending our own Legislatures, and declaring themselves invested with power to legislate for us in all cases whatsoever.

He has abdicated Government here, by declaring us out of his Protection and waging War against us.

He has plundered our seas, ravaged our Coasts, burnt our towns, and destroyed the Lives of our people.

He is at this time transporting large Armies of foreign Mercenaries to compleat the works of death, desolation and tyranny, already begun with circumstances of Cruelty & perfidy scarcely paralleled in the most barbarous ages, and totally unworthy the Head of a civilized nation.

He has constrained our fellow Citizens taken Captive on the high Seas to bear Arms against their Country, to become the executioners of their friends and Brethren, or to fall themselves by their Hands.

He has excited domestic insurrections amongst us, and has endeavoured to bring on the inhabitants of our frontiers, the merciless Indian Savages, whose known rule of warfare, is an undistinguished destruction of all ages, sexes and conditions.

In every stage of these Oppressions We have Petitioned for Redress in the most humble terms: Our repeated Petitions have been answered only by repeated injury. A Prince, whose character is thus marked by every act which may define a Tyrant, is unfit to be the ruler of a free people.

Nor have We been wanting in attentions to our Brittish brethren. We have warned them from time to time of attempts by their legislature to extend an unwarrantable jurisdiction over us. We have reminded them of the circumstances of our emigration and settlement here. We have appealed to their native justice and magnanimity, and we have conjured them by the ties of our common kindred to disavow these usurpations, which, would inevitably interrupt our connections and correspondence. They too have been deaf to the voice of justice and of consanguinity. We must, therefore, acquiesce in the necessity, which denounces our Separation, and hold them, as we hold the rest of mankind, Enemies in War, in Peace Friends.

We, therefore, the Representatives of the united States of America, in General Congress, Assembled, appealing to the Supreme Judge of the world for the rectitude of our intentions, do, in the Name, and by Authority of the good People of these Colonies, solemnly publish and declare, That these United Colonies are, and of Right ought to be Free and Independent States; that they are Absolved from all Allegiance to the

British Crown, and that all political connection between them and the State of Great Britain, is and ought to be totally dissolved; and that as Free and Independent States, they have full Power to levy War, conclude Peace, contract Alliances, establish Commerce, and to do all other Acts and Things which Independent States may of right do. And for the support of this Declaration, with a firm reliance on the protection of divine Providence, we mutually pledge to each other our Lives, our Fortunes and our sacred Honor.

John Hancock

	Wm. Hooper		Robt. Morris	Wm. Floyd	Josiah Bartlett
Button Gwinnett	Joseph Hewes,		Benjamin Rush	Phil. Livingston	Wm: Whipple
Lyman Hall	John Penn	Samuel Chase	Benja. Franklin	Frans. Lewis	Saml. Adams
Geo Walton.		Wm. Paca		Lewis Morris	John Adams
		Thos. Stone	John Morton		Robt. Treat Paine
		Charles Carroll of Carrollton	Geo Clymer		Elbridge Gerry
	Edward Rutledge.		Jas. Smith.		Step. Hopkins
			Geo. Taylor		William Ellery
	Thos. Heyward Junr.		James Wilson	Richd. Stockton	Roger Sherman
	Thomas Lynch Junr.	George Wythe	Geo. Ross	Jno Witherspoon	Saml. Huntington
	Arthur Middleton	Richard Henry Lee	Caesar Rodney	Fras. Hopkinson	Wm. Williams
		Th: Jefferson	Geo Read	John Hart	Oliver Wolcott
		Benja. Harrison	Tho M:Kean	Abra Clark	Matthew Thornton
		Thos. Nelson jr.			
		Francis Lightfoot Lee			
		Carter Braxton			

The names of four committee members charged with drafting the Declaration of Independence are shown in green. Robert R. Livingston, the fifth committee member, was called away from Philadelphia before the Declaration was signed.[18]

Hear All About It

John Hancock was President of the Continental Congress July 6, 1776, when he wrote General George Washington at Washington's New York headquarters:

> ...the Congress have judged it necessary to dissolve the Connection between Great Britain and the American Colonies, and to declare them free & independent States; as you will perceive by the enclosed Declaration, which I am directed to transmit to you, and to request you will have it proclaimed at the Head of the Army in the Way, you shall think most proper.[19]

In response to the letter,[20] Washington's July 9, 1776, General Orders to the Continental Army proclaimed:

> The Honorable the Continental Congress, impelled by the dictates of duty, policy and necessity, having been pleased to dissolve the Connection which subsisted between this Country, and Great Britain, and to declare the United Colonies of North America, free and independent STATES:

> The several brigades are to be drawn up this evening on their respective Parades, at six OClock, when the declaration of Congress, shewing the grounds & reasons of this measure, is to be read with an audible voice. The General hopes this important Event will serve as a fresh incentive to every officer, and soldier, to act with Fidelity and Courage, as knowing that now the peace and safety of his Country depends (under God) solely on the success of our arms:

And that he is now in the service of a State, possessed of sufficient power to reward his merit, and advance him to the highest Honors of a free Country.

The Brigade Majors are to receive, at the Adjutant Generals Office, several of the Declarations to be delivered to the Brigadiers General, and the Colonels of regiments.[21]

Samuel Blachley Webb, aide-de-camp to General Washington, wrote in his journal that the July 9, 1776, reading of the Declaration of Independence "…was received by three Huzzas from the Troops…"[22]

Focus on Facts

A six element demonstration is built on facts that intertwine with logic. Properly placed facts are usually the bulk of a six element demonstration. Logic binds the demonstration. Perfectly timed argument, Proof set up by facts, leads to a firm Conclusion.

Thomas Jefferson used the first part of the June 12, 1776, Virginia Declaration of Rights as a model for the Declaration of Independence Exposition. George Mason drafted the Virginia Declaration of Rights.

> A DECLARATION OF RIGHTS made by the Representatives of the good people of VIRGINIA, assembled in full and free Convention; which rights do pertain to them and their posterity, as the basis and foundation of Government.
>
> 1. That all men are by nature equally free and independent, and have certain inherent rights, of which, when they enter into a state of society, they cannot, by any compact, deprive or divest their posterity; namely, the enjoyment of life and liberty, with the means of acquiring and possessing property, and pursuing and obtaining happiness and safety.
>
> 2. That all power is vested in, and consequently derived from, the People; that magistrates are their trustees and servants, and at all times amenable to them.

3. That Government is, or ought to be, instituted for the common benefit, protection, and security of the people, nation, or community;—of all the various modes and forms of Government that is best which is capable of producing the greatest degree of happiness and safety, and is most effectually secured against the danger of mal-administration;—and that, whenever any Government shall be found inadequate or contrary to these purposes, a majority of the community hath an indubitable, unalienable, and indefeasible right, to reform, alter, or abolish it, in such manner as shall be judged most conducive to the publick weal...[23]

Thomas Jefferson wrote the preamble to the Virginia Constitution. Adopted on June 29, 1776,[24] Jefferson's third draft of the Virginia Constitution began:

A Bill for new-modelling the form of Government and for establishing the Fundamental principles thereof in future.

Whereas George Guelf king of Great Britain and Ireland and Elector of Hanover, heretofore entrusted with the exercise of the kingly office in this government hath endeavored to pervert the same into a detestable and insupportable tyranny;

by putting his negative on laws the most wholesome & necessary for ye. public good;

by denying to his governors permission to pass laws of immediate & pressing importance, unless suspended in their operation for his assent, and, when so suspended, neglecting to attend to them for many years;

by refusing to pass certain other laws, unless the persons to be benefited by them would relinquish the inestimable right of representation in the legislature

by dissolving legislative assemblies repeatedly and continually for opposing with manly firmness his invasions on the rights of the people;

when dissolved, by refusing to call others for a long space of time, thereby leaving the political system without any legislative head;

by endeavoring to prevent the population of our country, & for that purpose obstructing the laws for the naturalization of foreigners & raising the conditions of new appropriations of lands;

by keeping among us, in times of peace, standing armies & ships of war;

by affecting to render the military independent of & superior to the civil power;

by combining with others to subject us to a foreign jurisdiction, giving his assent to their pretended acts of legislation

for quartering large bodies of troops among us;
for cutting off our trade with all parts of the world;
for imposing taxes on us without our consent;
for depriving us of the benefits of trial by jury;
for transporting us beyond seas to be tried for pretended offences; and

for suspending our own legislatures & declaring themselves invested with power to legislate for us in all cases whatsoever;

by plundering our seas, ravaging our coasts, burning our towns and destroying the lives of our people;

by inciting insurrections of our fellow subjects with the allurements of forfeiture & confiscation

by prompting our negroes to rise in arms among us; those very negroes whom by an inhuman use of his negative he hath refused us permission to exclude by law

by endeavoring to bring on the inhabitants of our frontiers the merciless Indian savages, whose known rule of warfare is an undistinguished destruction of all ages, sexes, & conditions of existence;

by transporting at this time a large army of foreign mercenaries to compleat the works of death, desolation, & tyranny already begun with circumstances of cruelty & perfidy so unworthy the head of a civilized nation;

by answering our repeated petitions for redress with a repetition of injuries;

and finally by abandoning the helm of government and declaring us out of his allegiance & protection;

by which several acts of misrule the said George Guelf has forfeited the kingly office and has rendered it necessary for the preservation of the people that he should be immediately deposed from the same, and divested of all it's privileges, powers, & prerogatives...[25]

Jefferson's Virginia Constitution Preamble was a model for the Construction in the Declaration of Independence .

The opening phrase from Richard Henry Lee's June 7, 1776, resolution to the Continental Congress (see page 7, "Jefferson Made the Draft") became part of the Conclusion of the Declaration of Independence:

> That these United Colonies are, and of right ought to be, free and independent States, that they are absolved from all allegiance to the British Crown, and that all political connection between them and the State of Great Britain is, and ought to be, totally dissolved.[26]

The Greatest Question was Decided

July 3, 1776, John Adams wrote a letter to his wife Abigail. He described the passage of the resolution for independence by the Continental Congress:

> Yesterday the greatest Question was decided, which ever was debated in America, and a greater perhaps, never was or will be decided among Men. A Resolution was passed without one dissenting Colony "that these united Colonies, are, and of right ought to be free and independent States, and as such, they have, and of Right ought to have full Power to make War, conclude Peace, establish Commerce, and to do all the other Acts and Things, which other States may rightfully do." You will see in a few days a Declaration setting forth the Causes, which have impell'd Us to this mighty Revolution, and the Reasons which will justify it, in the Sight of God and Man.[27]

July 4, 1776, Delaware Continental Congress representative Caesar Rodney wrote a letter to his brother Thomas Rodney:

> I arrived in Congress (tho detained by thunder and Rain) time Enough to give my Voice in the matter of Independence. It is determined by the Thirteen United Colonies, without even one decenting Colony. We have now Got through with the Whole of the declaration, and Ordered it to be printed, so that you will soon have the pleasure of seeing it. Hand-bills of it will be printed, and sent to the Armies, Cities, County Towns etc…[28]

In 1816, Thomas Jefferson submitted corrections to his biography in *Public Characters of 1800-1801*. The corrections included, "I did not <u>propose</u> the declaration of Independence nor did I take any very leading part more than many others, to whom that merit equally belongs."[29]

In 1815, Philadelphia bookseller Joseph Delaplaine published *Delaplaine's Repository of the Lives and Portraits of Distinguished American Characters*. The book contained a chapter on Thomas Jefferson.[30] Jefferson's April 12, 1817, letter to Delaplaine clarified how modifications were made to the Declaration of Independence draft:

> your statements of the corrections of the Declaration of Independance by Dr Franklin and mr Adams, are neither of them at all exact. I should think it better to say generally that the rough draught was communicated to those two gentlemen, who, each of them made 2. or 3. short and verbal alterations only. but even this is laying more stress on mere composition than it merits; for that alone was mine; the sentiments were of all America.[31]

On August 30, 1823, Thomas Jefferson wrote James Madison regarding the Declaration of Independence, "I did not consider it as any part of my charge to invent new ideas altogether & to offer no sentiment which had ever been expressed before."[32]

In 1818, John Trumbull finished a 12 feet by 18 feet painting showing the June 28, 1776, drafting committee presentation of the Declaration of Independence to the Continental Congress. The painting was commissioned for the U.S. Capitol.[33] It was exhibited at Independence Hall in Philadelphia from 9 a.m. until dusk Tuesday, January 12, through Saturday, January 23, 1819, excluding Sunday, January 17.[34] In 1824, it was installed in the U.S. Capitol Rotunda.[35]

The Declaration of Independence initially was a smaller painting that Trumbull completed between 1786 and 1797.[36] This 20.875 inch by 31 inch painting is in the Yale University Art Gallery.[37] Trumbull based it on a sketch he made, and on a floor plan sketch "done by Mr. Jefferson in Paris 1786 to convey an Idea of the Room in which congress sat at the Declaration of Independence on the ground floor of the old State house in Philadelphia…"[38] Trumbull wrote in his autobiography:

> In the autumn of 1787, I again visited Paris, where I painted the portrait of Mr. Jefferson in the original small Declaration of Independence, Major General Ross in the small Sortie from Gibraltar, and the French officers in the Surrender of Lord Cornwallis, at Yorktown in Virginia. I regard these as the best of my small portraits; they were painted from the life, in Mr. Jefferson's house [The Hôtel de Langeac].[39]

U.S. Capitol

The Declaration of Independence, by John Trumbull

A December 28, 1817, letter from John Trumbull reminded Jefferson of Jefferson's 1786 assistance, and asked if he wanted to purchase prints of *The Declaration of Independence* painting.[40]

January 8, 1818, Jefferson responded:

> I can have no hesitation in placing my name on the roll of subscribers to the print of your Declaration of Independance, & I desire to do it for two copies. the advance of price from 18.66. to 20.D. cannot be objected to by any one because of the disproportionate decrease in the value of the money…while it is right to indulge the luxury of the rich with copies of exquisite & perfect execution would it not be worth your while to have one of mere outline engraved which could be sold for a dollar apiece? were such to be had, scarcely a hovel in the US. would be without one…[41]

Asher Brown Durand engraved the print. Dated 1820, the print was published in 1823.[42] A 21.875 inch by 30.375 inch brown tone print of Durand's *The Declaration of Independence* engraving hangs in Monticello's entrance hall.[43]

"I Cannot Live Without Books"

In an 1815 letter to John Adams, Thomas Jefferson wrote, "I cannot live without books…"[44] In the War of 1812, the British burned the U.S. Capitol. It contained the Library of Congress. Thomas Jefferson owned one of the best libraries in America. After the Capitol burned, he proposed to sell his library to Congress. Jefferson's library exceeded the size and scope of the original Library of Congress. It took him 50 years to acquire what he proposed to sell.[45]

January 26, 1815, the House of Representatives debated the bill to purchase Jefferson's library:

> Mr. King afterwards moved to recommit the bill to a select committee, with instructions to report a new section authorizing the Library Committee, as soon as said library shall be received at Washington, to select therefrom all books of an atheistical, irreligious, and immoral tendency, if any such there be, and send the same back to Mr. Jefferson without any expense to him. This motion Mr. K. thought proper afterwards to withdraw.

> This subject, and the various motions relative thereto, gave rise to a debate which lasted till the hour of adjournment; which, though it afforded much amusement to the auditors, would not interest the feelings or judgment of any reader.[46]

The House of Representatives approved the purchase of Jefferson's 6,487 volume library in a January 26, 1815, 81 to 71 vote. January 30, 1815, President James Madison signed the act to acquire Jefferson's library for $23,950.[47]

The purchase included books related to the six elements of a proposition: Euclid's *Elements*, and *The Philosophical and Mathematical Commentaries of Proclus on the First Book of Euclid's Elements*.[48] The definitions of the six elements were preserved by the fifth century philosopher Proclus.[49] Within the commentary, Proclus demarcated Euclid's Proposition 1 (the construction of an equilateral triangle) into the six elements of a proposition.[50]

Abraham Lincoln used the Library of Congress during his two-year Congressional term, 1847-1849.[51] In 1851, two-thirds of the books Congress purchased from Thomas Jefferson were destroyed in a fire.[52] The photographs on the next page were taken in November 2016 in the Library of Congress. The photographs show white box placeholders for missing Jefferson volumes. The Library of Congress continues to seek appropriate editions to fill in the original collection:

A Portion of Jefferson's Library

Euclid's *Elements*,[53] and Proclus'
Commentaries on Euclid[54]

The Masterpiece

The Declaration of Independence was a Thomas Jefferson masterpiece written according to the six elements of a proposition. We reviewed over 60 years of Thomas Jefferson's writings, including most of his 19,000 letters. We identified over 700 documents Jefferson wrote as persuasive demonstrations according to the six elements of a proposition. Many are beautiful and entertaining. Possibly none was more important than the Declaration.

On June 14, 1826, Washington Mayor Roger C. Weightman wrote Thomas Jefferson:

> As chairman of a committee appointed by the citizens of Washington to make arrangements for celebrating the fiftieth anniversary of American Independence in a manner worthy of the Metropolis of the nation, I am directed to invite you, as one of the signers of the ever memorable Declaration of the 4th of July 1776, to honor the city with your presence on the occasion.
>
> I am further instructed to inform you that, on receiving your acceptance of this invitation, a special deputation will be sent to accompany you from your residence to this city and back again to your home.[55]

June 24, 1826, ten days prior to his death, Thomas Jefferson wrote Mayor Weightman:

Enunciation: [**Given**] The kind invitation I recieve from you on the part of the citizens of the city of Washington, to be present with them at their celebration of the 50th. anniversary of American independance; as one of the surviving Signers of an instrument, pregnant with our own, and the fate of the world, is most flattering to myself, and heightened by the honorable accompaniment proposed for the comfort of such a journey. [**Sought**] it adds sensibly to the sufferings of sickness, to be deprived by it of a personal participation in the rejoicings of that day.

Exposition: but acquiescence is a duty, under circumstances not placed among those we are permitted to controul.

Specification: I should indeed, with peculiar delight, have met and exchanged there, congratulations personally, with the small band, the remnant of that host of worthies, who joined with us, on that day, in the bold and doubtful election we were to make, for our country, between submission, or the sword; and to have enjoyed with them the consolatory fact that our fellow citizens, after half a century of experience and prosperity, continue to approve the choice we made.

Construction: may it be to the world what I believe it will be, (to some parts sooner, to others later, but finally to all), the Signal of arousing men to burst the chains, under which Monkish ignorance and superstition had persuaded them to bind themselves, and to assume the blessings & security of self government. that form which we have substituted restores the free right to the unbounded exercise of reason and freedom of opinion.

all eyes are opened, or opening to the rights of man. the general spread of the light of science has already laid open to every view the palpable truth that the mass of mankind has not been born, with saddles on their backs, nor a favored few booted and spurred, ready to ride them legitimately, by the grace of god. these are grounds of hope for others. for ourselves let the annual return of this day, for ever refresh our recollections of these rights and an undiminished devotion to them.

Proof: I will ask permission here to express the pleasure with which I should have met my ancient neighbors of the city of Washington and of it's vicinities, with whom I passed so many years of a pleasing social intercourse; an intercourse which so much relieved the anxieties of the public cares, and left impressions so deeply engraved in my affections, as never to be forgotten.

Conclusion: with my regret that ill health forbids me the gratification of an acceptance, be pleased to recieve for yourself and those for whom you write the assurance of my highest respect and friendly attachments.[56]

From Monticello, in 1812, Thomas Jefferson wrote John Adams, "I have given up newspapers in exchange for Tacitus & Thucydides, for Newton & Euclid; & I find myself much the happier."[57]

From 1854 to his death, Abraham Lincoln was accomplished in the use of the six elements of a proposition.[58] In 1859, Lincoln wrote:

All honor to Jefferson—to the man who, in the concrete pressure of a struggle for national independence by a single people, had the coolness, forecast, and capacity to introduce into a merely revolutionary document, an abstract truth, applicable to all men and all times, and so to embalm it there, that to-day, and in all coming days, it shall be a rebuke and a stumbling-block to the very harbingers of re-appearing tyrany and oppression.[59]

President Lincoln borrowed from the Exposition of the Declaration of Independence for part of the Gettysburg Address Given: "all men are created equal."[60] In 1776, the survival of that principle as the basis of a nation was uncertain. On July 4, 1826, the 50th anniversary of the Declaration of Independence, John Adams and Thomas Jefferson both died.

The Declaration lives.

Adams Made the Argument to Congress

In 2004, Jefferson biographer and law professor R. B. Bernstein wrote, "All his life he [Jefferson] disliked public speaking; his voice was not suited to the task, and his shyness before a large gathering made any speech an ordeal."[61]

In 1822, John Adams observed:

> Mr. Jefferson came into Congress, in June, 1775, and brought with him a reputation for literature, science, and a happy talent of composition. Writings of his were handed about, remarkable for the peculiar felicity of expression. Though a silent member in Congress, he was...prompt, frank, explicit, and decisive upon committees and in conversation...[62]

President Abraham Lincoln commented in 1863:

> The two most distinguished men in the framing and support of the Declaration were Thomas Jefferson and John Adams—the one having penned it and the other sustained it the most forcibly in debate...[63]

From John Adams' autobiography:

The Committee of Independence, were Thomas Jefferson, John Adams, Benjamin Franklin, Roger Sherman and Robert R. Livingston. Mr. Jefferson had been now about a Year a Member of Congress, but had attended his Duty in the House but a very small part of the time and when there had never spoken in public: and during the whole Time I satt with him in Congress, I never heard him utter three Sentences together. The most of a Speech he ever made in my hearing was a gross insult on Religion, in one or two Sentences, for which I gave him immediately the Reprehension, which he richly merited.

It will naturally be enquired, how it happened that he was appointed on a Committee of such importance. There were more reasons than one. Mr. Jefferson had the Reputation of a masterly Pen. He had been chosen a Delegate in Virginia, in consequence of a very handsome public Paper which he had written for the House of Burgesses, which had given him the Character of a fine Writer. Another reason was that Mr. Richard Henry Lee was not beloved by the most of his Colleagues from Virginia and Mr. Jefferson was sett up to rival and supplant him. This could be done only by the Pen, for Mr. Jefferson could stand no competition with him or any one else in Elocution and public debate…

The Committee had several meetings, in which were proposed the Articles of which the Declaration was to consist, and minutes made of them. The Committee then appointed Mr. Jefferson and me, to draw them up in form, and cloath them in a proper Dress. The Sub Committee met, and considered the Minutes, making such Observations on them as then occurred: when Mr. Jefferson desired me to take them to my Lodgings and make the Draught. This I declined and gave several reasons for declining. 1. That he was a Virginian and I a Massachusettensian. 2. that he was a southern Man and

I a northern one. 3. That I had been so obnoxious for my early and constant Zeal in promoting the Measure, that any draught of mine, would undergo a more severe Scrutiny and Criticism in Congress, than one of his composition. 4thly and lastly and that would be reason enough if there were no other, I had a great Opinion of the Elegance of his pen and none at all of my own. I therefore insisted that no hesitation should be made on his part.

He accordingly took the Minutes and in a day or two produced to me his Draught. Whether I made or suggested any corrections I remember not. The Report was made to the Committee of five, by them examined, but whether altered or corrected in any thing I cannot recollect. But in substance at least it was reported to Congress where, after a severe Criticism, and striking out several of the most oratorical Paragraphs it was adopted on the fourth of July 1776, and published to the World.[64]

John Adams spoke strongly for the Declaration in Congressional debate.

Jefferson sat silent throughout the entire debate, so conscious of his weakness in oratory that he did not allow himself to defend the pet passages in his momentous document. The responsibility of presenting and sustaining the report of the committee was ably assumed by John Adams, whom Jefferson gratefully called "the Colossus" of that great debate.[65]

Daniel Webster, who voted against Congressional acquisition of Jefferson's library,[66] wrote that Thomas Jefferson told him in 1824:

John Adams was our Colossus on the floor [for passage of the Declaration]. He was not graceful, nor elegant, nor remarkably fluent; but he came out occasionally with a power of thought & expression, that moved us from our seats.[67]

In the House of Representatives on October 19, 1826, United States Attorney General William Wirt, eulogizing Jefferson and Adams,[68] described Jefferson's voice:

It is true he [Jefferson] was not distinguished in popular debate; why he was not so, has often been matter of surprise to those who have seen his eloquence on paper, and heard it in conversation. He had all the attributes of the mind, and the heart, and the soul, which are essential to eloquence of the highest order.

The only defect was a physical one: he wanted volume and compass of voice for a large deliberative assembly; and his voice, from the excess of his sensibility, instead of rising with his feelings and conceptions, sunk under their pressure, and became guttural and inarticulate. The consciousness of this infirmity repressed any attempt in a large body, in which he knew he must fail...[69]

Among Jefferson's books the Library of Congress bought in 1815 were 34 titles on rhetoric and oration.[70] In 1829, over two and a half years after his death, Jefferson's rebuilt personal library was auctioned. It included 20 titles on rhetoric and oration.[71] Books could not change the physical:

Jefferson's voice was weak and husky and he was never able to raise it above the tone of ordinary conversation; he was not fluent when upon his feet; there was no fire nor magnetism in his presence...[72]

These were the events of framer Thomas Jefferson and debater John Adams that resulted in the drafting and the passage of the American Declaration of Independence. Six elements ignited a fire in 1776.

Timeline

1743	Thomas Jefferson born.
1760-1762	Jefferson studied at William and Mary.
1762-1765	Jefferson studied law. George Wythe was his tutor.
1766-1771	Jefferson was a justice of the Albemarle County Court.
1766-1774	Jefferson was an attorney.
1769-1774	Jefferson was a member of Virginia House of Burgesses.
1775	Revolutionary War began.
1775-1776	Jefferson was a member of the Continental Congress.
Jun 7, 1776	Richard Henry Lee proposed a Continental Congress resolution for national independence.
Jun 11, 1776	Thomas Jefferson was appointed to a five person committee to draft the Declaration of Independence.

Jun 12, 1776	George Mason's Virginia Declaration of Rights adopted by the Fifth Virginia Convention in Williamsburg, Virginia.
Jun 29, 1776	Virginia Constitution containing Thomas Jefferson's preamble adopted.
Jul 2, 1776	Continental Congress approved Richard Henry Lee's resolution for independence from Great Britain.
Jul 3, 1776	John Adams wrote Abigail Adams describing the resolution for independence.
Jul 4, 1776	Continental Congress approved the Declaration of Independence.
Jul 9, 1776	General Washington ordered the Declaration of Independence to be read to the Continental Army.
Feb 12, 1809	Abraham Lincoln born.
Jan 30, 1815	Thomas Jefferson sold most of his library to Congress.
Aug 6, 1822	John Adams wrote Timothy Pickering to explain Thomas Jefferson's selection to draft the Declaration of Independence.
May 8, 1825	Thomas Jefferson's letter to Henry Lee described the Declaration's purpose.

Jul 4, 1826	Thomas Jefferson and John Adams died on the 50th anniversary of the Declaration of Independence.
1847-1849	Abraham Lincoln, a member of the Whig Party, served as a member of the House of Representatives in the 30th U.S. Congress.
Nov 19, 1863	Abraham Lincoln began the Gettysburg Address: "Four score and seven years ago our fathers brought forth on this continent, a new nation, conceived in Liberty, and dedicated to the proposition that all men are created equal."
1918	Ohio Supreme Court Judge R. M. Wanamaker, in *The Voice of Lincoln*, stated the Declaration of Independence has three parts: declaration, demonstration, and dedication.
1954	Jefferson historian Dumas Malone stated the Declaration of Independence has four parts: "a preamble, a philosophical paragraph, a list of charges against the King, and at the end the actual declaration of independence..."
2010	*Abraham Lincoln and the Structure of Reason* demonstrated Thomas Jefferson structured the Declaration of Independence according to the six elements of a proposition: Enunciation, Exposition, Specification, Construction, Proof, and Conclusion.

Endnotes

1. United States Continental Congress, "Friday, June 7, 1776," *Journals of the Continental Congress 1774-1789, Volume V. 1776* (Washington: Government Printing Office, 1906), 425.

2. United States Continental Congress, "Tuesday, June 11, 1776," *Journals of the Continental Congress 1774-1789, Volume V. 1776* (Washington: Government Printing Office, 1906), 431.

3. "Pickering, Timothy," *Biographical Directory of the American Congress 1774-2005* (Washington, D. C.: United States Government Printing Office, 2005), 1736.

4. John Adams, "To Timothy Pickering, August 6, 1822," *The Works of John Adams, Second President of the United States*, ed. Charles Francis Adams (Boston, MA: Little, Brown, and Company, 1865), 2:514.

5. David Hirsch and Dan Van Haften, "The Structure of Reason," www.thestructureofreason.com/home/how-the-discoveries-were-made (accessed July 11, 2016).

6. R. M. Wanamaker, *The Voice of Lincoln* (New York, NY: Charles Scribner's Sons, 1918), 130; for a description of Judge Wanamaker's reasoning concerning the three parts, see 215-217.

7. David Hirsch and Dan Van Haften, *Abraham Lincoln and the Structure of Reason* (El Dorado Hills, CA: Savas Beatie, 2010); See also www.thestructureofreason.com/home/how-the-discoveries-were-made.

8. Dumas Malone, *The Story of the Declaration of Independence* (New York, NY: Oxford University Press, 1954), 86.

9. John Ciardi, *How Does a Poem Mean?* (Boston, MA: Houghton Mifflin Company, 1959), 663-664.

10. John Ciardi, *How Does a Poem Mean?* (Boston, MA: Houghton Mifflin Company, 1959), 920.

11. Proclus, *A Commentary on the First Book of Euclid's Elements, Translated with Introduction and Notes by Glenn R. Morrow* (Princeton, NJ: Princeton University Press, 1970), 159.

12. Proclus, *A Commentary on the First Book of Euclid's Elements, Translated with Introduction and Notes by Glenn R. Morrow* (Princeton, NJ: Princeton University Press, 1970), 159.

13. Proclus, *A Commentary on the First Book of Euclid's Elements, Translated with Introduction and Notes by Glenn R. Morrow* (Princeton, NJ: Princeton University Press, 1970), 159.

14. Proclus, *A Commentary on the First Book of Euclid's Elements, Translated with Introduction and Notes by Glenn R. Morrow* (Princeton, NJ: Princeton University Press, 1970), 159.

15. Proclus, *A Commentary on the First Book of Euclid's Elements, Translated with Introduction and Notes by Glenn R. Morrow* (Princeton, NJ: Princeton University Press, 1970), 159.

16. Proclus, *A Commentary on the First Book of Euclid's Elements, Translated with Introduction and Notes by Glenn R. Morrow* (Princeton, NJ: Princeton University Press, 1970), 159.

17. Thomas Jefferson, "The Declaration of Independence, July 4, 1776," *The Papers of Thomas Jefferson*, ed. Julian P. Boyd (Princeton, NJ: Princeton University Press, 1950), 1:429-432.

18. "Livingston, Robert R.," *Biographical Directory of the United States Congress 1774-2005* (Washington, D.C.: United States Government Printing Office, 2005), 1457.

19. John Hancock, "John Hancock to George Washington, July 6, 1776," *The Papers of George Washington: Revolutionary War Series*, eds. W. W. Abbot and Dorothy Twohig (Charlottesville, VA: University Press of Virginia, 1993), 5:219.

20. George Washington, "To John Hancock, July 10, 1776," *The Papers of George Washington: Revolutionary War Series*, eds. W. W. Abbot and Dorothy Twohig (Charlottesville, VA: University Press of Virginia, 1993), 5:258.

21. George Washington, "General Orders, July 9, 1776," *The Papers of George Washington: Revolutionary War Series*, eds. W. W. Abbot and Dorothy Twohig (Charlottesville, VA: University Press of Virginia, 1993), 5:246.

22. Samuel Blachley Webb, *Correspondence and Journals of Samuel Blachley Webb*, ed. Worthington Chauncey Ford (Lancaster, PA: Wickersham Press, 1893), 1:153.

23. George Mason, "Virginia Declaration of Rights, June 12, 1776," *The Papers of George Mason, 1725-1792*, ed. Robert A. Rutland (Chapel Hill, NC: The University of North Carolina Press, 1970), 1:287.

24. Julian P. Boyd, ed. "The Virginia Constitution as Adopted by the Convention, [June 29, 1776]," *The Papers of Thomas Jefferson* (Princeton, NJ: Princeton University Press, 1950), 1:377-383.

25. Thomas Jefferson, "The Virginia Constitution, Third Draft [Before June 13, 1776]," *The Papers of Thomas Jefferson*, ed. Julian P. Boyd (Princeton, NJ: Princeton University Press, 1950), 1:356-357.

26. United States Continental Congress, "Friday, June 7, 1776," *Journals of the Continental Congress 1774-1789, Volume V. 1776* (Washington: Government Printing Office, 1906), 425.

27. John Adams, "To Abigail Adams, July 3, 1776," *Adams Family Correspondence*, ed. L. H. Butterfield (Cambridge, MA: The Belknap Press of Harvard University Press, 1963), 2:27-28.

28. Edmund C. Burnett, ed., "Caesar Rodney to Thomas Rodney, July 4, 1776," *Letters of Members of the Continental Congress* (Washington, D.C.: The Carnegie Institution of Washington, 1921), 1:528.

29. Thomas Jefferson, "Corrections to Biography in *Public Characters*, circa June 3, 1816," *The Papers of Thomas Jefferson: Retirement Series*, ed. J. Jefferson Looney (Princeton, NJ: Princeton University Press, 2013), 10:114.

30. Joseph Delaplaine, *Delaplaine's Repository of the Lives and Portraits of Distinguished American Characters* (Philadelphia, PA: Rogers & Esler Printers, 1815), 1:125-155.

31. Thomas Jefferson, "To Joseph Delaplaine, April 12, 1817," *The Papers of Thomas Jefferson: Retirement Series*, ed. J. Jefferson Looney (Princeton, NJ: Princeton University Press, 2014), 11:252.

32. The Thomas Jefferson Papers, "Thomas Jefferson to James Madison, August 30, 1823," The Library of Congress, www.loc.gov/item/mtjbib024747 (accessed May 15, 2016).

33. David McCullough, et al., *Life, Liberty, and the Pursuit of Happiness: American Art from the Yale University Art Gallery* (New Haven, CT: Yale University Art Gallery in association with Yale University Press, 2008), 67, 87.

34. Theodore Sizer, ed., *The Autobiography of Colonel John Trumbull, Patriot-Artist, 1756-1843* (New Haven, CT: Yale University Press, 1953), 319.

35. Theodore Sizer, *The Works of Colonel John Trumbull: Artist of the American Revolution* (New Haven, CT: Yale University Press, 1967), Fig. 158.

36. Theodore Sizer, *The Works of Colonel John Trumbull: Artist of the American Revolution* (New Haven, CT: Yale University Press, 1967), Fig. 158.

37. David McCullough, et al., *Life, Liberty, and the Pursuit of Happiness: American Art from the Yale University Art Gallery* (New Haven, CT: Yale University Art Gallery in association with Yale University Press, 2008), 87.

38. Julian P. Boyd, ed., *The Papers of Thomas Jefferson* (Princeton, NJ: Princeton University Press, 1954), 10:xxvii, 179.

39. John Trumbull, *The Autobiography of Colonel John Trumbull, Patriot-Artist, 1756-1843*, ed. Theodore Sizer (New Haven, CT: Yale University Press, 1953), 152.

40. John Trumbull, "John Trumbull to Thomas Jefferson, December 28, 1817," *The Papers of Thomas Jefferson: Retirement Series*, ed. J. Jefferson Looney (Princeton, NJ: Princeton University Press, 2015), 12:282-283.

41. Thomas Jefferson, "To John Trumbull, January 8, 1818," *The Papers of Thomas Jefferson: Retirement Series*, ed. J. Jefferson Looney (Princeton, NJ: Princeton University Press, 2015), 12:340.

42. Theodore Sizer, *The Works of Colonel John Trumbull: Artist of the American Revolution* (New Haven, CT: Yale University Press, 1967), Fig. 158.

43. Th Jefferson Monticello, "The House: Rooms and Furnishings, Hall," Thomas Jefferson Foundation, www.monticello.org/site/house-and-gardens/declaration-independence-trumbull-engraving (accessed February 15, 2017).

44. Thomas Jefferson, "To John Adams, June 10, 1815," *The Papers of Thomas Jefferson: Retirement Series*, ed. J. Jefferson Looney (Princeton, NJ: Princeton University Press, 2011), 8:523.

45. James Conaway, *America's Library: The Story of the Library of Congress 1800-2000* (New Haven, CT: Yale University Press, 2000), 27-28.

46. United States Congress, *The Debates and Proceedings in the Congress of the United States: Thirteenth Congress - Third Session* (Washington: Gales and Seaton, 1854), 1105.

47. United States Congress, *The Debates and Proceedings in the Congress of the United States: Thirteenth Congress - Third Session* (Washington: Gales and Seaton, 1854), 1105; James Conaway, *America's Library: The Story of the Library of Congress 1800-2000* (New Haven, CT: Yale University Press, 2000), 30; Richard Peters, ed., "Thirteenth Congress, Session III, Chapter XXVII.—*An Act to authorize the purchase of the library of Thomas Jefferson, late President of the United States.*," *The Public Statutes at Large of the United States of America* (Boston, MA: Charles C. Little and James Brown, 1846), 3:195.

48. James Gilreath and Douglas L. Wilson, eds., *Thomas Jefferson's Library: A Catalog with the Entries in His Own Order* (Washington, D.C.: Library of Congress, 1989), 94.

49. Proclus, *A Commentary on the First Book of Euclid's Elements, Translated with Introduction and Notes by Glenn R. Morrow* (Princeton, NJ: Princeton University Press, 1970), 159.

50. Proclus, *A Commentary on the First Book of Euclid's Elements, Translated with Introduction and Notes by Glenn R. Morrow* (Princeton, NJ: Princeton University Press, 1970), 162-164.

51. Douglas L. Wilson, *Lincoln before Washington: New Perspectives on the Illinois Years* (Urbana, IL: University of Illinois Press, 1997), 3; Earl S. Miers, ed., "Abraham Lincoln 1809-1848," *Lincoln Day by Day: A Chronology*

1809-1865 (Dayton, OH: Morningside, 1991), 324; Earl S. Miers, ed., "Abraham Lincoln 1849-1860," *Lincoln Day by Day: A Chronology 1809-1865* (Dayton, OH: Morningside, 1991), 8.

52. James Conaway, *America's Library: The Story of the Library of Congress 1800-2000* (New Haven, CT: Yale University Press, 2000), 46.

53. Library of Congress Catalog Record, *"The Elements of Euclid,"* The Library of Congress, lccn.loc.gov/03021837 (accessed January 29, 2017).

54. Library of Congress Catalog Record, *"The Philosophical and Mathematical Commentaries of Proclus on the first book of Euclid's Elements,"* The Library of Congress, lccn.loc.gov/03020865 (accessed January 29, 2017).

55. The Thomas Jefferson Papers, "Roger C. Weightman to Thomas Jefferson, June 14, 1826," The Library of Congress, www.loc.gov/item/mtjbib024898/ (accessed August 14, 2016).

56. The Thomas Jefferson Papers, "Thomas Jefferson to Roger C. Weightman, June 24, 1826," The Library of Congress, www.loc.gov/item/mtjbib024904 (accessed August 13, 2016).

57. Thomas Jefferson, "To John Adams, January 21, 1812," *The Papers of Thomas Jefferson: Retirement Series*, ed. J. Jefferson Looney (Princeton, NJ: Princeton University Press, 2007), 4:429.

58. David Hirsch and Dan Van Haften, *Abraham Lincoln and the Structure of Reason* (El Dorado Hills, CA: Savas Beatie, 2010).

59. Abraham Lincoln, "To Henry L. Pierce and Others, April 6, 1859," *The Collected Works of Abraham Lincoln,* ed. Roy P. Basler (New Brunswick, NJ: Rutgers University Press, 1953) 3:376.

60. David Hirsch and Dan Van Haften, *The Ultimate Guide to the Gettysburg Address* (El Dorado Hills, CA: Savas Beatie, 2016), 16.

61. R. B. Bernstein, *Thomas Jefferson: The Revolution of Ideas* (New York, NY: Oxford University Press, 2004), 30.

62. John Adams, "To Timothy Pickering, August 6, 1822," *The Works of John Adams, Second President of the United States: with A Life of the Author, Notes and Illustrations, by his Grandson, Charles Francis Adams. Vol. II* (Boston, MA: Little, Brown, and Company, 1865), 513-514.

63. Abraham Lincoln, "Response to a Serenade, July 7, 1863," *The Collected Works of Abraham Lincoln*, ed. Roy P. Basler (New Brunswick, NJ: Rutgers University Press, 1953), 6:319-320.

64. John Adams, *Diary and Autobiography of John Adams*, ed. L. H. Butterfield (Cambridge, MA: The Belknap Press of Harvard University Press, 1961), 3:335-337.

65. William Eleroy Curtis, *Thomas Jefferson* (Philadelphia, PA: J. B. Lippincott Company, 1901), 136.

66. United States Congress, *The Debates and Proceedings in the Congress of the United States: Thirteenth Congress - Third Session* (Washington: Gales and Seaton, 1854), 1106.

67. Daniel Webster, "Notes of Mr. Jefferson's Conversation 1824 at Monticello, 1825, *The Papers of Daniel Webster: Correspondence, Volume 1 1798-1824*, ed Charles M. Wiltse (Hanover, NH: University Press of New England, 1974), 375.

68. William Wirt, *A Discourse on the Lives and Characters of Thomas Jefferson and John Adams, Who Both Died on the Fourth of July, 1826* (Washington: Gales & Seaton, 1826), 1.

69. William Wirt, *A Discourse on the Lives and Characters of Thomas Jefferson and John Adams, Who Both Died on the Fourth of July, 1826* (Washington: Gales & Seaton, 1826), 28-29.

70. James Gilreath and Douglas L. Wilson, eds., *Thomas Jefferson's Library: A Catalog with the Entries in His Own Order* (Washington: Library of Congress, 1989), 124-125.

71. Nathaniel P. Poor, *Catalogue. President Jefferson's Library: A Catalogue of the extensive and valuable Library of the late President Jefferson* (Washington: Gales and Seaton, 1829), 13.

72. William Eleroy Curtis, *Thomas Jefferson* (Philadelphia, PA: J. B. Lippincott Company, 1901), 130.

Index

Abraham Lincoln and the Structure of Reason, structure of Declaration of Independence, 60

Adams, Abigail, 41, 59

Adams, John, 59; member of committee to draft Declaration of Independence, 1, 54; letter to Timothy Pickering, 1-2; letter to Abigail Adams, 41; letter from Thomas Jefferson, 46, 51; death, 52, 60; Declaration of Independence, 53, 56, 57; autobiography entry, 54-55; public speaking, 55; described by Thomas Jefferson, 56

Albemarle County Court, 58

argument, 5; proper timing, 21, 36; placement in Declaration of Independence, 23

Bernstein, R. B., on Thomas Jefferson as public speaker, 53

British, War of 1812, 46

Ciardi, John, 8

Conclusion, 36; within six element pyramid, 7; definition, 24; Declaration of Independence, 24-25, 40

Construction, within six element pyramid, 7; definition, 16; Declaration of Independence, 16-19, 40; sets up Proof, 17

Continental Congress, 1, 34, 58

Declaration of Independence, U.S. Capitol, 43-44; John Trumbull, 43-45

Declaration of Independence, committee to draft, 1, 54, 58; Jefferson selected to draft, 1-2, 54-55; six elements of a proposition, 3; six element pyramid structure, 5; understanding, 6; Enunciation, 10-11; Exposition, 12-13, 36; Specification, 14-15; Construction, 16-19, 40; Proof, 20-23; original document, 23; Conclusion, 24-25, 40; logical development, 26-27; colorized demarcation, 28-33; signers, 33; read to Continental Army, 35; approved by Continental Congress, 41, 59; Jefferson's view of, 42; not proposed by Thomas Jefferson, 42; celebration of, 49; use by Abraham Lincoln in Gettysburg Address, 52

Delaplaine, Joseph, 42

Durand, Asher Brown, 45

elements of a proposition, six element pyramid structure, 7

Enunciation, within six element pyramid, 7; definition, 10; Declaration of Independence, 10-11

Euclid, 51

Euclid's *Elements*, 47, 48

Exposition, within six element pyramid, 7; definition, 12; Declaration of Independence, 12-13, 36

facts, Given, 11, 27; Exposition, 13, 27; Construction, 17, 27; Declaration of Independence, 36-40

factual foundation, 5; placement within the six elements, 27, 36

fire, 57; argument, 5; "burnt our towns", 19, 31; "burning our towns", 39; U.S. Capitol burned by British, 46; 1851 Library of Congress, 47

Franklin, Benjamin, member of committee to draft Declaration of Independence, 54

Gettysburg Address, 60; Given, 52

Given, within six element pyramid, 7; Declaration of Independence, 10-11

Hancock, John, letter to George Washington, 34

House of Representatives, debate on acquisition of Thomas Jefferson's library, 46

How Does a Poem Mean?, 8

hypothesis, 4, 25, 27; Specification, 15; Proof, 22

Jefferson, Thomas, member of committee to draft Declaration of Independence, 1, 54, 58; selected to draft Declaration of Independence, 1-2, 54-55; writing skill, 2, 53, 55, 56; use of the six elements of a proposition, 3, 49; use of Virginia Declaration of Rights, 36; Virginia Constitution preamble author, 37; Declaration of Independence Conclusion, 40; included in *Public Characters of 1800-1801*, 42; letter to James Madison, 42; letter to Joseph Delaplaine, 42; letter to John Trumbull, 45; letter to John Adams, 46, 51; sale of personal library to Library of Congress, 46-47, 59; letter to Roger C. Weightman, 50-51; praised by Abraham Lincoln, 51-52; death, 52, 60; Declaration of Independence, 53, 57; public speaking, 53, 55; voice, 53, 55, 56; rhetoric books in library at death, 56; birth, 58; studied law, 58

Lee, Henry, 59

Lee, Richard Henry, resolution for independence, 1, 40, 58

Library of Congress, acquisition of Thomas Jefferson's library, 46-47; 1851 fire, 47

Lincoln, Abraham, study of Declaration of Independence, 3; use of six elements of a proposition, 3; member of U.S. Congress, 47, 60; praise for Thomas Jefferson, 51-52; Gettysburg Address, 52, 60; on Declaration of Independence, 53

Livingston, Robert R., 33; member of committee to draft Declaration of Independence, 54 location, importance of, 36

logical development, Declaration of Independence, 26-27; Sought, Specification, and Conclusion, 27

logical direction, 5

Madison, James, letter from Thomas Jefferson, 42; signed act to acquire Jefferson's library, 47

Malone, Dumas, structure of Declaration of Independence, 4, 60

Mason, George, Virginia Declaration of Rights, 36-37, 59

Philosophical and Mathematical Commentaries of Proclus on the First Book of Euclid's Elements, 47, 48

Pickering, Timothy, letter from John Adams, 1-2, 59

poetry, meaning of, 8

Proclus, commentary on Euclid, 47, 48

Proof, 36; within six element pyramid, 7; definition, 20; Declaration of Independence, 20-23; argument, 21

Public Characters of 1800-1801, Thomas Jefferson's corrections, 42

resolution for independence, 1; Declaration of Independence Conclusion, 40

Rodney, Caesar, letter to Thomas Rodney, 41

Sherman, Roger, member of committee to draft Declaration of Independence, 54

six elements of a proposition, Abraham Lincoln's use of, 3; Declaration of Independence, 3; Thomas Jefferson's use of, 3; Euclid's Proposition 1, 47

Sought, within six element pyramid, 7; Declaration of Independence, 10-11; statement of general issue, 11

Specification, within six element pyramid, 7; definition, 14; Declaration of Independence, 14-15; contrasted with Sought, 15

structure of Declaration of Independence, R. M. Wanamaker, 3, 60; Dumas Malone, 4, 60; *Abraham Lincoln and the Structure of Reason*, 60

Trumbull, John, *Declaration of Independence*, 43-45

U.S. Capitol, *Declaration of Independence*, 43-44

Virginia Constitution, Thomas Jefferson's preamble, 37-40, 59

Virginia Declaration of Rights, 36-37, 59

Voice of Lincoln, 3, 60

Wanamaker, R. M., structure of Declaration of Independence, 3, 60

War of 1812, 46

Washington, George, General Orders, 34-35

Webb, Samuel Blachley, 35

Webster, Daniel, 55

Weightman, Roger C., letter to Thomas Jefferson, 49

William and Mary, 58

Wirt, William, eulogy of Adams and Jefferson, 56; on Thomas Jefferson as public speaker, 56

The Authors

David Hirsch is an attorney in Des Moines, Iowa. He has a BS from Michigan State University and a JD, with distinction, from the University of Iowa College of Law. He clerked for an Iowa Supreme Court Justice from 1973-1974. In addition to a diversified "small town" law practice, Hirsch was a columnist for the *American Bar Association Journal* for over a decade. Hirsch is admitted to practice in all Iowa state trial and appellate courts, plus: United States Supreme Court, United States Court of Appeals for the Eighth Circuit, United States District Court for the Southern District of Iowa, United States District Court for the Northern District of Iowa, United States Court of Claims, United States Tax Court.

Dan Van Haften lives in Batavia, Illinois. He has BS, with high honor, and MS degrees in mathematics from Michigan State University, and a Ph.D. in electrical engineering from Stevens Institute of Technology. He began his career with AT&T Bell Laboratories in 1970, and retired from Alcatel-Lucent in 2007. He worked on telecommunication software development and system testing. He presently writes full time.

Visit their website: www.thestructureofreason.com.

Other Books by David Hirsch and Dan Van Haften

The Ultimate Guide to the Gettysburg Address

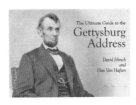

"The authors in their deconstruction of Lincoln's Gettysburg declaration have helped make it a looking glass for America. David Hirsch and Dan Van Haften deserve commendation for their continued analysis of Lincoln's literary work through the 'Structure of Reason.' Always illuminating, the authors discuss the six elements of a proposition; enunciation, exposition, specification, construction, proof, and conclusion in language that we can all understand. It is another great contribution to the Lincoln bibliography."

— **Frank J. Williams**, Chair, The Lincoln Forum, and
retired Chief Justice of the Rhode Island Supreme Court

"Once again, Hirsch and Van Haften illuminate a signal strength of Lincoln's rhetoric, and thus of his legacy: his careful yet simple construction of reasoned speech. The influence of Lincoln, and the influence of the duo's first book upon current political figures, is now demonstrated as well. This new volume is another remarkable achievement."

— **James Cornelius**, Curator of the Lincoln Collection,
Abraham Lincoln Presidential Library & Museum

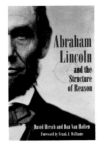

Abraham Lincoln and the Structure of Reason

"[O]ne of the most stunningly original works on Abraham Lincoln to appear in years…Hirsch and Van Haften show us how Lincoln applied the Euclidean logic of geometry to the language of law and politics."

— **John Stauffer**, Harvard University English and History Professor